A Day at Nanny and Eddy's

Josée Lavoie

Today, Eloise and her family are travelling to visit her grandparents, Nanny and Eddy.

They live in a little blue house in a village named Moonbeam.

"Hi Nanny, Eddy and Jake!" says Eloise.

"**Hi sunshine!**" says Nanny.

"**Hello Eloise!**" says Eddy.

"**Woof!**" says Jake.

Eloise loves when Nanny calls her sunshine.
It makes her feel warm and happy.

"Should we make some soup?" asks Nanny.

"Yes! Let's make some tasty soup with veggies from the garden!" says Eloise.

Eddy tends to their beautiful vegetable garden with a lot of patience...

... and he chases away the squirrels to keep them from nibbling on their veggies.

"Which vegetables should we harvest for today's yummy soup?" asks Eddy.

"**We have a rainbow of veggies for our little sunshine's soup!**" says Eddy.

"**I'm so excited to show Nanny!**" says Eloise.

This is what they put in the basket:

With her basket full, Eloise is excited to start cooking the soup with Nanny.

"Great choice of vegetables!" says Nanny.

Eloise cleans all of the veggies with Nanny. She watches Nanny chop the carrots, onions, celery and tomatoes. Then, Eloise puts all of the veggies in the casserole.

Once all of the vegetables are soft, Nanny adds them to a big pot of chicken broth.

It already smells yummy!

While they wait, Eloise and Nanny look at old family photo albums.

"That's your daddy when he was little with his dog Tippy." says Nanny.

Eloise draws pictures of owls because those are Nanny's favourite birds.

They dance to Nanny's favourite songs.

The smell of the yummy soup
fills the entire little blue house.

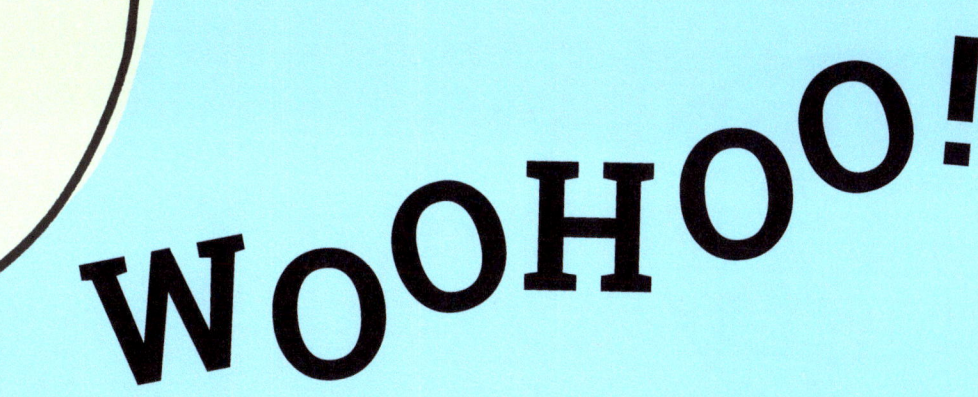

WOOHOO!

Lunch is ready.

Everyone sits around the table to enjoy the tasty soup full of Eddy's vegetables, Nanny's love and Eloise's help.

...Even Jake!

To my loving grandparents, Nanny & Eddy.
I'll always be your little sunshine.

Copyright © 2023 by Josée Lavoie

All rights reserved. The translation or reproduction of any excerpt of this book in any manner whatsoever, either electronically or mechanically and, more specifically, by photocopy and/or microfilm, is forbidden.

A Day at Nanny and Eddy's
© Text by Josée Lavoie. 2023
© Illustrations by Josée Lavoie. 2023

Published by Josée Lavoie

HeyJosee.com

ISBN:
978-1-990829-02-4 (Hardcover)
978-1-990829-06-2 (eBook)

First Edition, 2023

www.ingramcontent.com/pod-product-compliance
Lightning Source LLC
Chambersburg PA
CBHW041404010526
44107CB00015B/1064